OAKLAND COMMUNITY COLLEGE

3 2355 00110679 8
PS 3523 .O344 S6   OCHL
Spring of the

D1060893

PS
3523
.O 344
S6

Logan

Spring of the thief

Oakland Community College
Highland Lakes Library
7350 Cooley Lake Road
Union Lake, Michigan

OTHER BOOKS BY

JOHN LOGAN

POETRY: *Cycle for Mother Cabrini* (1955)
Ghosts of the Heart (1960)

FOR CHILDREN: *Tom Savage* (1962)

SPRING OF THE THIEF

SPRING
OF THE THIEF

POEMS
1960–1962

BY

JOHN LOGAN

NEW YORK

ALFRED · A · KNOPF

1963

L. C. catalog card number: 63-14350

THIS IS A BORZOI BOOK
PUBLISHED BY ALFRED A. KNOPF INC.

Copyright © 1960, 1961, 1962, 1963 by John Logan. All rights reserved. No part of this book may be reproduced in any form without permission in writing from the publisher, except by a reviewer, who may quote brief passages in a review to be printed in a magazine or newspaper. Manufactured in the United States of America, and distributed by Random House, Inc. Published simultaneously in Toronto, Canada, by Random House of Canada, Limited.

FIRST EDITION

THE following two poems are reprinted by permission: "To a Young Poet Who Fled," first published in *Mutiny Magazine*, copyright © 1961 by Mutiny Press; and "Whistling Wings," first published in *Poetry Northwest*, copyright © 1963 by Poetry Northwest.

FOR

C S C
A   E
S S

THE REDEMPTION HAS HAPPENED.

THE HOLY GHOST IS IN MEN.

THE ART IS TO HELP MEN

BECOME WHAT THEY REALLY ARE.

Most of these poems first appeared in the following magazines, to whose editors acknowledgment and thanks are due: *Audience, Big Table, Chicago Choice, The Commonweal, The Critic, Evergreen Review, Literary Review, Minnesota Review, Mutiny, Paris Review, Poetry Dial, Poetry Northwest, The Sixties, Sewanee Review, Spokesman, Statements.*

CONTENTS

[vii

PART

I

MONOLOGUES OF THE SON
OF SAUL

I

Ah so, our first load of honey heavy Christmas trees.
Then the sweet Christ comes again. See, in the high truck bed
the greens spring easy as the thighs of young lovers
while the aromatic golden gum, gift of The Magus,
oozes under the light cover of snow, rising slow
as the milk of the dead. Mothers will survive these rites
of birth, it is said. We prove it by our liturgy.
But I do not believe my own theory, and am cursed
to figure how I was blest at the root of my heart
by a man sitting underneath a flowering tree
in a white shirt open at the throat, dark face lucid,
saying the stories of a father for me. Yet I,
I have thieved my father's treasure. And I cannot pay.
On my naked birthday I brought to bed his amber haired,
shy eyed wife, her face birch white against the linen
loaf or coif of her pillow. Now, Advent, her quilted,
copper coffin glows again with a green, harlot's light
inside my head. Oh I've tried boyishly before today to lay her virgin ghost in this enormous house,
but still I feel her black teeth click and push at the roots
of its dying blood (or apple) colored bush.

II

I did but taste a little of the honey with the
tip of my rod and my eyes were opened, and behold
I must die. May God do so and more my father said
for thou shalt surely die, Jonathan, but the Lord God
sent leaping from the heart of a bush a saving ram,
and so I live. Oh I have not my father's wisdom,
gift of a tender God to strike me blind in the road
and send me wandering, goodly monomaniac,
all one-eyed, over the oceans of Odysseus
(while my wife's fingers bleed as breasts on her unfinished
      web).
Yet though I have not my father's light I would know
my fault. For I did but taste a little of the honey
with the tip of my rod. Through God my life was knit
to his who killed the giant king with a stalk he ground
into the single, brazen eye: showering his blood
like rays of lucid wine watering the green slips of men.
I loved him as my own soul. I took off my clothes
and gave them to him, even my sword and bow and belt.
See, I have made myself naked for my brother. I
have made myself poor. Later when my jealous father
spoke to him alone at the table and had him play
the melancholy lute in his room, I loved him more
it seemed and took his part before the throne of Saul. Then
suddenly my father saw him enemy and sought
his life, the hot young breath of David, who won his wife
with foreskins of a thousand dead. When my father threw
the javelin at him, he fled. God what was his fault?
We sat at meat. I felt the cold growing in my groin
when my father cried for him, and so I lied for love
till my father called my mother whore and threw the spear
at me! It struck the wall. What was his fault then, or mine,
David's friend, who shot my arrow past the barren shelf
where he hid and turned the wrath of Saul against myself?
Out of a place toward the south my brother rose and

4]

falling to the ground bowed himself thrice. He kissed my
        face.
We wept together for our human need, praying God
forever be between him and me, and among our springing
        seed,
for we but tasted honey in the summer wood.

III

"Far off the road on the left on a slight rolling hill"
I cannot eat my son in the tower of the barn
black with rain, though I lie on my back and starve to death
in a dirty shirt, sick and pierced in the flank by spears
of bronze straw, where he sits beside, his curious eyes
open in the dark, having twice dressed with rags my sweat-
tossed nakedness as I tore slobbering at my sack.
Christ I wish my sin in the barn had me drunk with wine!
Or that I lay in my chains looked at by gentle guards—
muscled, grizzled, Roman hero stripped and left to starve.
If a brown-eyed woman came to the barn in the long
rain, shivering with wet, child folded at her big breast,
I was too weak to talk. My son told I vomited
his stolen bread six days, even when he chewed and fed
the pap for me. (I know he cried as a child who tried
to keep alive some enormous feeble bird he had.)
No money to buy his milk, he said. I heard her breath,
felt her glance along my naked leg, and then away.
She sat hunched and silent, child across her lap. She rose
at last, and sighed: "Wait. I have to dry my clothes. I'll
        keep
the coat." And gave my son her child, moving into the
smoking, summer shadow of the barn. As she undressed
ah my God I could not taste again our ancient sweet
yearning in the flesh, now soft as underthighs of frogs,
and thought I was already dead. I wept. She walked close
wrapped in her wool coat of wine red. I shook my head. Yet
she lay beside me on the crushed, yellow shoots of hay
as though to rest, and loosened on one side her gold breast,
full as pears the drunken bees tremble for in the fall. She
drew down my giant skull. There, she said. There.
And I felt her fingers stir, weaving their life in my hair.

6]

IV

In my dream I know I see my father Saul a king,
the bronze gates of home shot open with a ram of oak,
my parents' private rooms naked to the look of the
enemy, cleats of their tough boots clacking in the halls,
packing the doors, where the mothers cling and seem to kiss
the wooden jambs in the hope of saints. The inner house
stirs with cries. The court shunts toward the cope of sky
          (and its
cold stars) the women's keening. Fifty bridal chambers,
extravagant boast for his children's children, their doors
thick with spoils of carved barbaric gold, smoke to ruin.
My father fastens round his aged, shivering breast
the dull arms of his youth, binds on his sword and sheath
and bends toward his death. See, beneath the open dark sky
a massive rock altar by a years-old laurel tree
that holds all of our loved household gods in its shadow.
My mother and sisters hover at the altar stones,
as doves driven by the hot storms, clutching husks of gods,
and when they see the king dressed in his rust streaked armor
Mother scolds him for his madness, asking where he goes
and sits him down softly by the sacred lights to pray.
Suddenly along the echoing colonnades my
screaming brother runs the gantlet of the enemy!
Chased by a mocking giant hacking at his young limbs
with swords. He circles through the court and long rooms and
          comes
last, moaning, before my parents' altar to pour his life
in pools as wasted semen or sacramental wine
shattered on the stone. My father cries that he has lived
to see his sons bled before his eyes like slaughtered pigs.
He curses my brother's murderer and flings his spear. It
rings the shield weakly, sticks and droops from the bronze
          belly.

The giant drags my father to the altar, shaking
and obscenely sliding in the blood of family—
he twists the old hair in his left hand, raises his red
sword in the right, and buries it in my father's heart.
My father does not die a death of fame. His white head-
less trunk rolls on the shore without a name.

V

If the half moon stamp of a sacred hoof showed Cadmus
where to found the town of Thebes, so what: Medea's love
has left me Corinth, as she careens into the sun,
her murdered kin (I think again of that hot, young niece
I had in bed) like a white and awkward albatross
about her neck—or like the dead ducks of poets, stretched
across a virgin lap. She fled mad in a flame red
chariot knit with copulating snakes, as the fake
staffs of medicine, rods of Mercury or Aaron
(whose brother came to life again out of a box a-
mid the holy human grass). It was this scene of snakes
god damned Tiresias to his female half of life!
So then my sweet son Bellerophon do not play mad
as David did, fellow in your art, who let his wife
lower him out of the house in a wicker cart. Oh,
I know how Saul himself (no artist) foamed in the mouth
and lay down nude all one day and night to prophesy
when David cut his shirt privily—he who played out
on the melancholy lute psalms of every man's heart.
The lame and ugly son of Jonathan, father dead,
and ignorant of his father's friend, sweat like a girl
to David's face, without faith the king had ever loved
in his youth, or first possessed the poet's gentle curse.
Oh my well loved son Bellerophon, you too have reined
the winged horse—your bastard brother Odysseus
lurked inside a wooden one, and waited to be born.
You would not stone as him the martyr Greek or wander
over his ancient, arrogant, labyrinthine route.
Odysseus I got on the daughter of a thief.
(The little, burnt moons I branded on the cattle's foot
printed down the road toward her house). Odysseus
was goared when he visited the crook, and you like him
are lame my son and beg for your poor bread, pushed at last
off the back of soaring Pegasus, who now is walked—
a tender-eared ass!—to pack the thunderbolts of Zeus.

[9

You fell into a bramble bush like a horny saint
to blind your looking eyes and break the legs you dance on.
Yet no more than Orpheus or drowning Arion
could you escape the women, and one you had refused
lied like the wife of Potiphar—once you shot with lead
the disconsolate Chimera's female jaw, whose hot
breath smoked and began to melt the ore down her sucking
      maw.
Ah son, on the moaning beach Xanthian bitch on bitch
mad with juice they took from the smears of mares in rut,
      ran
at you, lifting up their skirts, to cut your manly parts!
For they hoped a poet's blood would fountain in their wombs
and make them quick. See, I weep for you my eunuch son,
beloved Bellerophon, and up the mound roll
back again the gradual rock of my grieving heart.

February 1960

TO A YOUNG POET WHO FLED

> *Your cries make us afraid, but we love*
> *your delicious music!*
> —KIERKEGAARD

So you said you'd go home to work on your father's farm.
We've talked of how it is the poet alone can touch
with words, but I would touch you with my hand, my lost son,
to say good-bye again. You left some work, and have gone.
You don't know what you mean. Oh, not to me as a son,
for I have others. Perhaps too many. I cannot
answer all the letters. If I seem to brag, I add
I know how to shatter an image of the father
(twice have tried to end the yearning of an orphan son,
but opened up in him, and in me, another wound).
No—I say this: you don't know the reason of your gift.
It's not the suffering. Others have that. The gift of tears
is the hope of saints, Monica again and Austin.
I mean the gift of the structure of a poet's jaw,
which makes the mask that's cut out of the flesh of his face
a megaphone—as with the goat clad Greeks—to ampli-
fy the light gestures of his soul toward the high stone seats.
The magic of the mouth that can melt to tears the rock
of hearts. I mean the wand of tongues that charms the exile
of listeners into a bond of brothers, breaking
down the lines of lead that separate a man from a
man, and the husbands from their wives, in these old, burned
        glass
panels of our lives. The poet's jaw has its tongue ripped

as Philomel, its lips split (and kissed beside the grave),
the jawbone patched and cracked with fists and then with
      the salve
of his fellows. If they make him bellow, like a slave
cooked inside the ancient, brass bull, still that small machine
inside its throat makes music for an emperor's guest
out of his cries. Thus his curse: the poet cannot weep
but with a public and musical grief, and he laughs
with the joys of others. Yet, when the lean blessings come,
they are sweet, and great. My son, I could not make your
      choice.
Let me take your hand. I am too old or young to say,
"I'd rather be a swineherd in the hut, understood
by swine, than be a poet misunderstood by men."

PART

2

THE THIRTY-THREE RING CIRCUS

I

1

The wife of the clown,
a disconsolate performing goose,
is held by a rope
to a stake, like a hippopotamus.

2

The two and trio of hammer men,
torn dirty jeans and shirts,
poised black arms raised naked in the sun,
bow and gesture with the ancient grace
smashing iron stakes, in counter-
point of two or three strokes.

3

A carnival kid in white
cotton training pants
(perhaps the son of a gnome?)
is not spanked for fiddling with wires
at a socket on the shell of his home.

4

If we try to see in the curtains
of a performer's trailer, before
the circus, it is with the hope
of sneaking a look
at some slobbering freak.

5

An old, slop-hat, melancholy
father, no Telemachus found,
rushes weeping about the tent and ground.

6

The circus leopards start
electronic echoes.

7

The snake that can crush a pig
lies thick in a tank, its big
eye turning white, and its hide
which glowed with silver and red
on a sunshot Indian bank,
has begun to stink.

8

In the sawdust
nest of the ring
a small car spawns
a litter of clowns.

9

One grabs his hat and loses his pants
and grabs his pants and loses his hat
and grabs his hat and loses his self-
respect, his wife, and every mark
of his former art and life.

II

10

The elephant, ill with fatigue,
straws of its bed on its back,
nudges in the ring
with a kind of stupid tenderness.

11

The camel, improbable
on the face of the earth,
behind the glazing eyes
in its small skull a dream
of sand, has placed its hump
thru a hole in a flag
advertising salad oil.

12

Not even shot
from a cannon,
the clown shivers
inside, peeks o-
ver the rim and
throws out
his human hat.

13

The woman in a blue bustle,
man in a blue blouse,
are skating on some thin ice
at the top of the house.
(Zeus crashing to earth
would take his spouse.)

14

The man stands up
behind the woman who stands up
behind the boy who stands up
behind the child who stands
on the bench beside its mother.

15

The girl has lost her face.
It blurs with her brown hair
as her body spins a sheath,
by the skin of its teeth.

16

The drummer, belly sweating
thru his shirt, conducts
with ease an inane waltz
of death or life on the trapeze.

17

Two fairies teeter
on the high wire.
In despair one leaps
over the other,
breaks his fall, and swings
solo, head over tail.

18

The man with a white parasol
walks a rope (in a white
suit) sloped from the floor
to the top of the highest pole
in the tent, and vanishes
in a cloud of light at the vent.

19

The lion hides his dung
and swings under his flank
his leather genital
unable to pump the furious seed
in a steaming African glade.

20

A harem of a hundred girls,
lavender veiled, their navels
and tops of breasts exposed,
beautifully die
before the stands, and rise
on ropes to Mohammedan heaven
where they play in unison
their tiny xylophones.

21

The man who
stands on one
finger, on
one edge of
a ladder
on one leg,
on a ball,
tentative
as a soul.

III

22

Twirling her beads and plumes
she rears and jumps the horse
and tries to make him dance
(not a chance).

23

Unarmed a clown,
separated from the men
of his battalion,
is lost and shot down—
his dumb head blown clean
from his trunk. He trudges home
sorry and alone.

24
The giddy ostrich man
with his huge, orange ass
and bent bodice, his neck
hairy and slim (a gift
ribbon on its original apple),
scurries drunk and shy
avoiding our argus eye.

25
Clowns in adult, big feet,
red wigs and print dresses
with no hips
hang out their wash in the noon
August heat of the tent,
their sweating upper lips
hysterical with
hatred of their sons.

26
She swings out
into the audience
with swimming hair:
tights cuddling
graceful breasts,
her belly, and her
ravenous, universal
crotch—just
visible for an instant
above the crowd.

27

Black maned, the magnificent golden
Philippino, stripped to the waist, chest
oiled and smooth as a boy's, rides aloft
with his family. He takes the hand
of his wife, gliding past his brother,
who catches a perch and sweeps past him
to the wife, and they fly together
for a while till she exchanges them
in mid-air and he guides her again.
At last he turns toward his brother, and
throws a triple somersault, and fails, flop-
ping harmless into a nylon net.

28

Six ponies have burned
a circle into the ground
giving rides to kids.
(Their trainers trace
the radius.)

29

After the tent is down,
the circus owner, having
slept over, sets out
in his red car, feeding
his silver slug of a house
over the waste he is lord of.

30

Kids on bicycles
gathering bottles
and a dozen bent,
thirty-five-cent fans
from the Orient.

31

By a dead bon-
fire lies the charred
button down
shoe of a clown.

32

Between the well
and the hill
is the skull
of a doll.

33

So gored a thousand times through the heart
and mouth and thighs our earth smells of the death
of worlds, for the sulphur dung of Royal Bengal
tigers, the droppings of birds of paradise
and thin llamas from the rare plateaus
mingle on the local lot
with popcorn and the vomit of a dog.

HOMAGE TO CHRISTINA ROSSETTI

1

Christina (seven) skipped a stone
in a small pond by her home:
a frog came up from the dead
or sluggish waterweed, tossed

to his head (enormous eyed!)
his green and ivory hand
and moved away from there—with
A touching, still too human air.

2

If Christina found a dead bird
she would with pity bury it.
Once being tempted, bad and young
she came back to play a small God
uncovering the graceful mound,
but soon fled (crying) from a worm,
a thinner and more awful form.

3

"How she loved to catch a
    cold, little toad
or caterpillar

in the hollow of her
    beautiful hand,"
said Christina's friend.

4

A white peacock
on the Rossetti's lawn
    shook its gorgeous
watching plumes up and down,

    crying out with
sharp, inhuman pleasure.
    A fallow deer,
priestly, grace full creature,

    was overwhelmed—
and following the bird
    trampled each eye
tropical and absurd.

5

Christina received
    from her lover
who went down to sea
    in the summer

A gift for her house:
　　the small sea mouse
delicately haired
　　and colored green,

preserved in some wine.

6

When Christina turned sixteen
　　she began to dream:
it was Regent's Park at dawn
　　as the sun dropped down
its cold, almost moon-like light
　　shattering on the
stone to a rose or grey pond;
　　and through the clean sun,
through the blurred, green, naked limbs
　　of trees, suddenly

yellow waves of light are swept!
　　All the canaries
of London fly their cages
　　to flock in the spring-
chilled day's halfawakened trees,
　　their small ecstasies
letting undulating light
　　rise like an odor
from their lean, golden bodies
　　hovered together.

*For Marya Zaturenska in gratitude for
her book on Christina Rossetti*

PART

3

ON READING CAMUS
IN EARLY MARCH

I discovered inside myself, even in the very midst of winter, an invincible summer. —Camus

That boy in the red coat packing snow
mixes in my mind with the obscure
taste for beauty Camus's writing stirs.
I don't say the beauty of the boy—
open only through his naked face,
only his eyes drawing the full stores
of his emerging life, that seems to
root deeply back toward the dead. (See
how the boy stands footless in the snow,
like some smashed piece of Italian stone.)
Not that, but what he does to the cold,
pure seed or sand through his muffled hand:
how he brings the Midas touch of art—
I don't care how crude he seems to mold.
Not sad or old, not adult, the boy
has no more need of art than a saint;
and as he throws against the wall, shattering what his hand could form, I feel
the older, more yearning child's alarm.

SONG ON THE DREAD OF
A CHILL SPRING

I thought (and before it was too late)
my heart had begun to turn, that was
shut to love, for I was adamant
as saints, and tough as the martyr's heart,
as a wooden statue of a god,
where my father sat in the straight pew,
my mother bowed to the stone, bearing
flowers she had cut out of the earth
of my life. Ah the candles bloom cold
in the earthen air of early Mass,
like the tops of wan hepatica
that lift their light cups in the first time.
So shy we touch at these Ides of March!

Winter was too long and cold. The spring
is brief. These tulips offer up their gold
and the purple plum our grief.

LAMENT IN SPRING

Oh I have felt these same
yearnings in myself—
the tiny dark and yellow
hairs lit with wet
at the center of the May Day
violets Elizabeth held
in her seven-year-old fist
some six or seven years before
the grace she gave the afternoon

(her hand stemmed in mine)
at the topaz time of day
when children doze and she,
Elizabeth, waits breath-
less at the edge of the well.
She was my brother's girl,
and so I let her go.
For who can stand these old stirrings
in himself, and that one too?

LINES ON HIS BIRTHDAY

I was born on a street named Joy
of which I remember nothing,
but since I was a boy
I've looked for its lost turning.
Still I seem to hear my mother's cry
echo in the street of joy.
She was sick as Ruth for home
when I was born. My birth
took away my father's wife
and left me half
my life. Christ will my remorse
be less when my father's dead?
Or more. As Lincoln's minister of war
kept the body of his infant boy
in a silver coffin on his desk,
so I keep
in a small heirloom box of teak
the picture of my living father.
Or perhaps it is an image of myself
dead in this box she held?
I know her milk like ivory blood
still runs in my thick veins
and leaves in me an almost
lickerish taste for ghosts:
my mother's wan face,
full brown hair, the mammoth breast
death cuts off at the bone—
to which she draws her bow

again, brazen Amazon,
and aiming deadly as a saint
shoots her barb
of guilt into my game heart.

January 23, 1961

THE EXPERIMENT THAT FAILED

It is probable that mutual transfusions were first performed in 1492 between Pope Innocent VIII and two healthy boys, an experiment culminating in deaths of all concerned including the Pope.
—SOURCE BOOK OF ANIMAL BIOLOGY

I have not written my poem
about the Pope and the two young men
the obscure, muddle-headed muse
first sent when I first read
histories of the transfusion experiment.
And I do not know why,
except for the bitter fight
in me—about the fact
the boys died. (But so did he.)
The two youths look alike
in my thought. Though one is good,
one bad. Both are dead.
I may distinguish yet
between the dark and light.
One shouldn't have to kill them both.
What do we kill them with?
A knife and tourniquet?
A porcelain dish,
its white edge flecked with dirt
causing the blood to clot

34]

(so he demands more
from one or another)? A tube
of some fifteenth-century rubber?
God, the irony.
This was the time of discovery!
The very year the Catholic Columbus
tried for a splendid shore
in his three, piddling ships.
Together they made one—
Columbus was a man.
His Canary Island docking
was an imaginative mistaking.
But what can *I* find out?
I don't even know what killed them.
Or him. And I do not want
to think it was the loss of the blood
of manhood. There is always more of that.
Besides it is really feminine
to bleed and be afraid.
Well, what then?
The one old and the two young
men. Two fresh stones, or wells—
and the powerful, untried pen.
What cut them down?
Columbus ... Washington ... the mythical tree ...
the recurring blade. . . . No.
I don't see.
Yet my mind keeps holding back
with its bloody axe of stone
another idea
nobody wants known:
that it was the hope of a fresh, transmuted life
for which the Pope
and Columbus and the two sons died.

TALE OF A LATER LEANDER

*Great display guts. Fine young man
come from America swim Dardanelles
which had not seen daytime and espe-
cially this late in year. I say "Yashaa"
to this young man.*
        —TURKISH CAPTAIN QUOTED IN *Life*

1

If thieves got your bags at Istanbul
you flew across the sea of Marmara
and banged on the gates of the little shops
at dusk, hollering for aid. The minaret
of a mosque, gathering the last light,
glowed above the blue-and-gold mosaic arch
like the torch of Hero at her point of watch
high over the killing Hellespont.

2

You raised the dead to fill your need.
You rode over the rock strewn plain for hours
near Leander's mythical home, to climb
aboard a scow manned by a mad team
of Turks, veterans of the cold swim.
The ship's cabin was lighted by a single,
urine yellow lantern, and an old Greek
steered by hand her length of thirty-six feet.

3

Midnight beneath an ancient Asian moon
you strip to the heroic, gold muscle and bone,
smear your belly and chest, swollen sex
and flanks with the scow's own engine grease,
and like a naked dancer poise—to dive
into the heart cold sea, its water
dark with Shelley's or Leander's blood,
its waves lit with pearls of their spent seed.

4

Your foot feels for the bottom of their grave,
rich with the silt of poet's earth,
Edward King and Hart Crane, and of other
wanderers to the sea: sailor, coral,
dolphin, anemone. And you rise again,
flesh flashing white! and black! in the pharos'
broken light. Eyes haunting, intent,
you start to crawl across the Hellespont.

5

Soon your bones cool to the core, and your face
aches and changes in that awful chill.
You rest on your back playing the girl
to the current and the moon, and drift downstream,
until you hear the Turks scream gibberish
from the scow, and turn to fight with the sea
again, heading north to the Bosporous—
moved as Io dogged by the lust of Zeus.

6

Once I hear you groan, see you are gone
beneath the surface of a wave, one hand
caught around the big, quivering stone
of your leg, stroking it, caressing
it, as a lost boy, toward your heart,
and treading water like a broken bird,
one winged. Ah, melanchoy Icarus I feel
the sea's chill at the quick of my own skull.

7

Faintly they shout. You won't turn back
toward the ship, but drag your leg
as Jacob struggling with some abstract strength,
with Proteus, or the devil of the ice. Byron
circles his grotesque foot in the Hellespont—
as you watch the mouths of the madmen work
furious in the gaudy jets of light,
hearing how the cold has made you deaf!

8

A rope crawls on the skin of your back,
and you turn panic-struck into the phosphorous wake
of a black ship that bears its harrowing screw
just beyond, huge and spirit silent . . .
Weak as a tin boat you faint at last
on the rocks by the base of Hero's tower,
and the Turks haul up a frozen, shuddering, oily
beast of the sea: its twitching limbs still gesture
in the old, flesh-remembered motions of the swimmer.

PART

4

ON A PHOTOGRAPH
BY AARON SISKIND

> *Te Deum laudamus*
> *O Thou Hand of Fire!*
> —HART CRANE

1

After some miserable disaffection
of the only human heart and human hand
we'll ever have, we move to this pictured glove
or hand (ghostly absence) of Aaron Siskind,
a small spirit by image, able to shape

eloquently in the air—as though
to tell, "a man stands here"—able to meet
a handsome and beloved guest, or turn
so tenderly on a wife's face and breast.
Thus this glove, flecked with white paint that glints like

the unnatural light of an angel's scale
brushed off at Jacob's crippling, desperate fall . . .
pale froth on the wrist and palm of a proud youth . . .
or the pearls that whisper through the Doge's hand.
It is the left glove, the hand of The Magus,

of all who come late or by devious ways
oblique to honor Christ, all who have stopped
to see the sure, more customary king,
having set some ridiculous gift apart—
as frankincense or myrrh, gold for the child, art.

2

The glove's backed by grained wood
it is in some light held
molded at the lid
as the arm of a Saint in amber and glass
in another cast it rests
laid by with the love of a man
to be caught up again
or it will float out toward us from that rich wood
like the hand of him who draws life
deep into the massive limbs
of Adam gesturing
to name all the gorgeous animals of earth
I know it is this hand
or glove of God that teases us
so that we must change our life.

3

Yet in certain lights it is a melancholy hand
sloughed off with the body's green flesh. It is the stone
glove of Keats, its thumb and first finger fast angled
in that last, inexorable geometry,
unable to tell a quill or fix the rush of wine
that has made the reader mad and left him graced again,
his face caught in a gentle, momentary peace.
Ah Christ where is that grave hand this glove has left behind?
Once it held a brush heavy with the hope of beauty.

4

It is a hand that has already waved good-bye.
By it we know
we have missed our joy.
The glove is waste,
relic of a little work long since done.
The fingers bend stiff upon the palm
for it lay doubled on them as it dried,
a dead hand of Nietszche's dying god.
Ghost of the Master's hand!
Glove of Aaron Siskind! I
feel your canvas touch
flicked with lead spots of paint
upon the cold point of my heart.

This picture is a fist.
I feel it is a thing
Siskind had cut out of my quivering chest—
out of my huge, furred stomach.
It is a fist. It is a face
in the mirror I no longer watch;
and its light flecks have now the glint of tears
I have never wept
out of the tender, bald knuckles of my eyes.

A SUITE OF SIX PIECES
FOR SISKIND

1

A white notch as of bone
for a lost gun,
its prongs as roots
of a mammoth overturned tooth—

or like the odd feet
of some ultimate, melancholy freak—
looks into a profound honeycomb
the texture (odor?) of a morel mushroom.

2

The tip
of a leaf
is the wing of a bird
pinned (stretched) to a board.

3

A smashed piece of terracotta
shaped as the bottom
of a whale's mouth
(edges shorn of teeth)

stands upright
like a little, sacred shrine.
And on the shattered tongue
of this relic is

the impress of a stone chalice.

4
A glowing spi-
ral of white
paint

across a concrete post
or telephone pole
lights up this solemn, chalk tale:

I love mama.

5
Why a film of mud
blisters into the shape of a sun!
its black
rays like a baroque work

of sculpture seem to shiver
when an ancient,
fair cloth
is stripped off.

6

A luminous, thin
long winged worm

or trout
like an animal of light

swims into the deep humours of my eye
bringing this fish pale day.

EIGHT POEMS ON PORTRAITS
OF THE FOOT

(After Aaron Siskind)

1

It is the wish
for some genuine change other than our death
that lets us feel (with the fingers of mind)
how much the foot desires to be a hand.

The foot is more secret, more obscene,
its beauty more difficultly won—
is thick with skin and
so is more ashamed than the hand.

One nestled in the arched back of the other
is like a lover
trying to learn to love.
A squid or a slug, hope still alive

inside its mute flesh
for the grace and speed of a fish.
Sperm in the womb quickens to a man.
The man yearns toward his poem.

2

With its over-long
profile lines of bone
and dark stem at the top
this African foot

is an avocado turning sweet,
or a hand-carved, upturned boat.
An idol carved of ebony wood.
I weave before it in the sand.

3

The broad, high palm tap-
ered, with its top
toes shadowed into a ridge

is like a hooded figure.
I find I don't want to picture
underneath that cloak

the hidden face of the foot.

4

One thick
foot is fixed
across another like an ancient

occult monument
of basalt
all of its meaning lost.

5

At the top of crossed foot branches
two rows or bunches
of small, fat birds are hunched.
Somehow they manage to touch

with tenderness. Short,
bundled up, squat
peasants,
they begin to dance.

6

One humped
foot, heel up,
lolls heavily on another.

Feet are members of a natural pair
and on these
(left and right)

sand has the glint of wheat.

7

The turned toes
in a rococo
scroll together form
continuing curves, one last line

after another,
with a final spiral of vapor
(or of light)
beyond that.

8

Held toward a water colored sky
full of birds and gods and souls
of the young,
the whole, lyrical foot bal-

ances, with its heel
on the great toe of its mate.
Watch! Next that earthen foot
will step into flight!

PART

5

THE WOODEN MIRROR

*For if anyone is a hearer of the word,
and not a doer, he is like a man looking at his natural face in a mirror; for
he beholds himself and goes away, and
presently he forgets what kind of man
he was.* —Epistle,
FIFTH SUNDAY AFTER EASTER

I wait beside the fount.
My God whispers in the box
where a fellow sinner still confesses.
Again my mind caresses
with my hand the iron fence
that protects or that ornaments,
out of art, caution or some
paradigmal wisdom,
the dish kept for our baptism.
I had forgot this fount
has eight sides of highly rubbed wood,
each with a Gothic arch in relief
leading nowhere
but to my own natural face
shadowed in its mirror.
Yet I could not forget
between these trips, as grace
wings more niggardly
(or simply goes) this
pressed, iron rose

black as the hope of the melancholy
brother to our sins, who spent
all his beautiful coins of light—
and heavy as a body
whirled through the dark
outer petals of our world. . . .
The voice of the father
a little louder
as he absolves inside his cell
is like the gentle dropping of a waterfall.
God this grill is tall as I!
This oaken pedestal and base
as many-faced.
See the brass opening in the wood
where the priest may turn his ancient key?
The line of penitents shifts
to me. Christ I know this shut,
double-locked fount
is like the hidden basin of my heart
inside its guard of ribs and skin.
Bless me Father for I have sinned
against love,
and now near middle age,
hang guilty on the rods of my own cage.

LINES FOR HIS SON IN SATIN

*The tragic hero is a man afraid of his
own beauty.*
　　　　　　—GORDON QUINLAN, STUDENT

So my son I would have given my right arm
to have carried the queen's train
with a gloved hand, when I was young—
the queen up ahead, me
unafraid, in a blue satin suit
my grandmother made, and tennis shoes of new white,
white knee sox, a fancy mesh in them,
and a blue silk hat with an ostrich plume!
But what would I have done
if like you I had to find my place alone
(because a page can't mix
with others present
for the Virgin's crowning pageant)?
I doubt I could have sat in the pew
with such grace as you,
full of my absolute duty
and calm with the sense of my own beauty
luminous as stone, with a blue stone's light,
my solemn, sweet page.
Let me show you a picture of me
at your age. This boy is handsome too.
His arms drop with ease. But look close.
See how his brown hair, light as a girl's,

too fine to comb down in the small wind,
pushes against the side of his head
as though it were caved in
by some forgotten chance,
and the tight cotton pants banded at the knees,
as are yours, above the calves bare to the touch of grass,
the young genital full against the leg.
But why is there such a rage in his face?
A mere boy standing in the summer grass
caught there with a boy's grace. . . .
My son, page, I feel you bear a message
to me (though I am no king)
like a magnificent, blue stone ring upon a pillow
or a courtier's melancholy song:
that it is this very youth himself,
the summer wind and grass
gentle at his legs and face,
whom the boy's brown eye hates—
for though he wears no satin suit
or thin page's glove, he has
too much beauty, and can win easy
too much love.

REVISIT TO THE ROOM
OF A SAINT*

Yesterday in Chicago for the moment
penitent, vigilant for her ancient feast,
I visited her place of death
and found the blood of a saint she left
on the flesh colored mat
beside her tiny bed. What a doll she was.
Even her roll-top desk
with its postal scale seems small.
Her letter opener, paper clips, picture of The **Pope,**
blotter—and the folded, remarkable
eyeglass and ruler! I wanted to touch her gold-
topped pencil like my father's
but could only slip a finger
under the edge of the celluloid cover.
And there's a celluloid box
around the little, lifeless wicker chair
where she rocked
her self into the better air.
Beside the saint's spoon and cup
and her final clothes
are her ugly little shoes.
They stand without a step inside a glass case
skin cracked from twenty-seven trips over seas
and once over the angular, ivory
Andes. Her small, folded linens

* The Shrine of St. Francis Xavier Cabrini in Columbus Hospital,
Chicago.

have in them an aura of the gold mountain sun,
of fresh opened earth, of firs and rain,
the odors of The Virgin Queen.
A thing she wore, a kind of sleeveless shirt,
is feathered at the edges
as with lace, or with the brush
of her tiny bones as she moved,
habited and in her black
crochet-tipped hat or coif
over the earth, like an earth-bound little bird.
White doves wound above the field at her birth.
Now wine, gold, and turquoise doves
rise surely for her death. Their tissue wings
thin and lucid as her light hands
make a light wind.
Let it breathe on my hidden face
as my beast
kneels a moment in this child's place.

December 22–25, 1961

SPRING OF THE THIEF

But if I look the ice is gone from the lake
and the altered air
no longer fills with the small
terrible bodies of the snow.
Only once these late winter weeks
the dying flakes
fell instead as manna or as wedding rice
blooming in the light
about the bronze Christ
and the thieves. There these three
still hang, more than man-
sized and heavier than life
on a hill over the lake
where I walk
this Third Sunday of Lent.
I come from Mass
melancholy at its ancient story
of the unclean ghost
a man thought he'd lost.
It came back into his well-swept house
and at the final state that man
was worse than he began.
Yet again today
there is the faintest edge of green
to trees about St. Joseph's Lake.
Ah God if our confessions show contempt
because we let them free us of our guilt
to sin again

forgive us still . . . before the leaves . . .
before the leaves have formed
you can glimpse the Christ and Thieves
on top of the hill. One of them was saved.
That day the snow had seemed to drop like grace
upon the four of us,
or like the peace of intercourse,
suddenly I wanted to confess—
or simply talk.
I paid a visit to the mammoth Sacred Heart
Church, and found it shut.
Who locked him out or in?
Is the name of God changing in our time?
What is his winter name?
Where was his winter home.
Oh I've kept my love to myself before.
Even those ducks weave down the shore
together, drunk with hope
for the April water. One spring festival
near here I stripped and strolled
through a rain filled field.
Spread eagled on the soaking earth
I let the rain
move its audible little hands
gently on my skin . . . let the dark rain
raise up my love.
But why? I was alone
and no one saw how ardent I grew.
And when I rolled naked in the snow one night
as St. Francis with his Brother Ass
or a hard bodied Finn
I was alone. Underneath
the howling January moon
I knelt and dug my fist
full of the cold winter sand
and rubbed and

hid my manhood under it.
Washed up at some ancient or half-heroic shore
I was ashamed that I was naked there.
Before Nausicaä and the saints. Before myself.
But who took off my coat? Who put it on?
Who drove me home?
Blessed be sin if it teaches men shame.
Yet because of it we cannot talk
and I am separated from myself.
So what is all this reveling in snow and rain?
Or in the summer sun when the heavy gold
body weeps with joy or grief or love?
When we speak of God, is it God we speak of?
Perhaps his winter home
is in that field where I rolled or ran . . .
this hill where once the snow
fell serene as rain.
Oh I have walked around the lake
when I was not alone—
sometimes with my wife have seen these swans
dip down their necks
graceful as a girl, showering white and wet!
I've seen their heads delicately turn.
Have gone sailing with my quiet, older son.
And once on a morning walk
a student who had just come back
in fall found a perfect hickory shell
among the bronze and red
leaves and purple flowers of the time
and put its white bread into my hand.
Ekelöf said there is a freshness
nothing can destroy in us—
not even we ourselves.
Perhaps that
Freshness is the changed name of God.
Where all the monsters also hide

I bear him in the ocean of my blood
and in the pulp of my enormous head.
He lives beneath the unkempt potter's grass
of my belly and chest.
I feel his terrible, aged heart
moving under mine . . . can see the shadows
of the gorgeous light
that plays at the edges of his giant eye . . .
or tell the faint press and hum
of his eternal pool of sperm.
Like sandalwood! *Like sandalwood*
the righteous man
perfumes the axe that falls on him.
The cords of elm, of cedar oak and pine
will pile again in fall.
The ribs and pockets of the barns will swell.
Winds and fires in the field rage
and again burn out each
of the ancient roots.
Again at last the late November snow
will fill those fields, change this hill,
throw these figures in relief
and raining on them
will transform
the bronze Christ's brow and cheek,
the white face and thigh of the thief.

March–April, 1962

PART

6

WHISTLING WINGS

OR

WHITE TURTLE IN THE WATERTREE

1

"Whistling Wings." Jesus Christ.
Can you imagine that?
We thought we were so smart.
Had the turtle in a cage
for birds, till I couldn't stand the image
longer. Then we thought
the copper mesh around his pen would always flop
him back again
when he reached a certain point of compensation.
Like a youngster on a birch
he crawled up, catching each improbable turtle foot
(which the limbs of doves and wrens reflect).
But we must admit he won. He's gone.
Myth of the eternal return!
Perhaps he carries the world upon his flank again:
When we climbed up the back of Castle Rock
to take a long, leisurely look
all the maiden hair fern
shivered in the sun,
and the dry sweet pine
scales snapped like crusts of bread.
I felt the turtle's great wing shudder overhead.

Then again I saw the clams
try to put out wings
of a whitish meat (like small, phlegmatic souls)
from the Sisyphean shells
they always bear
even though abandoned in an auto tire.

The lean frog fled too.
Oh, we knew
he'd never feast upon the sun
blasted grass one kid put in,
wouldn't like the tone
of weeds against his precious slime.
Still we had a right to hope
he'd like the shallow hole
we dug, with its hand made pool.
But the frog's not anybody's fool.
Now (or thus)
as with Breughel's Icarus
I can see, in the green flowing
of my mind, his white, human legs flashing!
They leave a melancholy ring
like the abandoned whipporwill's song.

He starts up at nine o'clock
each heartbreaking night.
The partridge has some sadness or other
knocking softly in his throat as a missing motor,
but the whipporwill's music is the shadow, is the moon
of the last sheen of light in the meadow after rain.

66]

The field itself leaves us blest
in an unrelieved length of pine forest—
like the baroque squiggle in the sand
of baby clams
toward water,
track of partridge with the cock's delicate trailing feather,
or turtle's print before (and after)
the shore has smoothed with weather.

2
Off the pine path
we found a pair of grey clad
wood cutters (work shirts and pants,
heavy hats
to keep off bugs and sun)
whose nagging saws had broke the peace of the afternoon.
The kids and I watched them
hack an arm
and leg from trees they'd felled.
"Pulp" I've heard the living trees called!
I held
my breath when one took off his hat
to mop the sweat
and suddenly instead a woman was there,
her hair
falling round a rather pretty face
gaunt with tiredness—
and in her blue, metallic eyes, as in a cage,
an absolute feminine rage.

There was masculine fury
at the Inn just off the highway
(like the inn of Joseph and Mary,
as the natives tell)
where a husband sent six Indians to hell.

The man and his wife, who had two daughters,
were the tavern owners.
He took the wagon into town for salt and bread,
came back to find his wife and daughters dead!
Four Indians had killed them with a tomahawk,
robbed the inn and were quickly drunk.
The husband slew the four
with an axe right there,
brought two more back
and placed six heads about the inn on pikes!
Now they have a marker at a wayside park.

3
With my own wife and kids
visiting the local Indian burial grounds
I find I wonder
at the penny-strewn boxes stretching over
graves recently dug
for Billy Walking Bird and Nora White Dog.
I would guess
a kind of halfway house?
They are buried on a low, wooded hill
where blue grass seed and plum blossoms fall.

In another small area of cleared wood
across a net like that our turtle had
the kids hit a plastic badminton bird.

On a rope outside our concrete block cabin,
clean and damp and open
the many colored swimming suits sway,
all shapeless after joy.
At the beach, girl is clearly girl and boy, boy.
The motor boats buck across the lake
and root about the skirts of sails, who walk
by so slow
and turn so delicately now

A blue and red and yellow and brown
and green and black paper chain
my daughter makes
to drape
across the drab stove in the corner,
each color repeating in a perfect order.
Yet this doesn't make plain to me
her genuine, womanly intensity.
See how she
bangs and shatters the dinner bell!
Which here is on a pole.
The house or cabin key now hangs upon a hook
over the kitchen sink.
These new juxtaposings make you think!
The baby's crib's back by our bed again,
and the other kids—blankets fluffed and clean,
shook from plexiglass bags—
all are rearranged.

4

At Whistling Wings our oldest son
gets up early to fish, for the first time,
or stands gold with summer sun
plumed in a gaudy summer shirt
like a splendid, tropical bird
none of us know,
to draw back his brand new bow
and shoot forever
the first slim arrow of my quiver.

That one late night,
only a hint
or moonlight,
Ruth and I
(our children all asleep)
ran down from the cabin to the beach
and dived together
naked in the summer water.
I asked her out to swim with me because
I knew how small and white she was.

His hair too long and yellow for the wood
the baby walks
quite drunk,
or else bending back
on heels like a pregnant lady
round and round a small tree,
or like a cub bear,
paws clumsy in the air,
nosing honey,
or like a grounded baby bumble bee.

Our young son Stephen looks
like a small anchor seated on the stoop,
his back to me, knees drawn up
and spread, arms hid
at some uncertain game he made.

5

I have seen them strain and wheeze
to pull down young shoots of trees
they carry before them,
tiny dying limbs
held out,
as they circle slow and chant,
like elaborate candelabra in a rite.
(Once I thought
I saw my kids carried in their own trees,
parked there like ancient, shrieking harpies.)
And once in a low fog that rolled toward the wood
like those long sighs of the dead
I saw my charmed kids
conjure up or lose a voice, an arm, a head.

The girls put a puppet together
out of cork, sticks, string, and a feather.
They painted gentle or horrendous masks
full length on paper cleaning sacks.
And I have seen them push
or wish
a full cardboard carton
like a wagon
up a hill of sand,
and down at last
into the sweet valley of grass.
Have watched the boys build
a blunt sloop of board
and make it sail!
Saw one pound a nail
in a tin squash can
and tie fish line
to make a toy filled with stone
he dragged all around the cabin
yard.
Then (though I was gone) I've heard
our eleven-year-old
pulled an eighteen-pound
carp on a clothesline
straight down the main street in town
to weigh it in at the grocery store scale.
(Small, external Jonah. Revised whale.)
Once they nailed a brown bullhead
to a board
(through the snout)
and worked out his guts
having peeled off
the skin, like a man's sox
with pliers from my toolbox.
And they say the whole business is orthodox!

72]

6

Except for the littlest one
all my sons
and I went out to fish one night.
Couldn't wait
to try a new lure,
sweet little thing from France we thought of her:
La Vivif.
No Jitterbug, no Cisco Kid or River Thief,
or black or flesh colored rubber worm
to bring the small mouth bass home,
a weedless hook hid
inside its dull head.
Blue, red, bronze, and cream shapely *La Vivif*
would bring more beautiful strife.
We walked from the cabin east
toward the Ghost
for whom the boys had named the trail,
which leads to the water for a mile.
In the dead night walking near
we were startled by a startled deer!
Then, past a turn, at a sudden quirk,
that Ghost showed up in the germinating dark
hovering in the limbs of a ginkgo tree,
its great awkward silver body
like a snagged cloud
or enormous bird,
faintly glinting in the thin moon.
If it was a wounded weather balloon,
I felt it could still detect
the climate of my heart.
We joked too much (as they play
with bones on Corpus Christi Day).
Past the balloon, bird, cloud, or ghoul
we came to the walleye hole.

Putting that Vivif to the test
almost at the first cast
a good pike
flashed out of the lake!
I let each boy touch
the pole to feel the fish's tug,
and fought and landed it
luminous and foam wet,
the great eye without a lid
perhaps alive, perhaps dead.
Drunk with the success of our allure,
following some heady, ancient spoor
of ourselves or it
the older boys and I quickly stripped and fell
into the cold, walleye hole,
like shining gold
bugs or clumsy newborn birds
hopping from a black limb (abandoned nest and shell)
into a blue black pool.
I hit a snag of weed,
was caught like an anxious white turtle hid
in the branches of the water's trees
for a long minute of time,
then dressed and went home.

Necedah, Wisconsin
Summers: 1961–1962

A NOTE ABOUT THE AUTHOR

JOHN LOGAN was born in Red Oak, Iowa, in 1923. He received his B.A. in zoology from Coe College and his M.A. in English from the University of Iowa, and has done graduate work in philosophy at Georgetown University and Notre Dame. He has taught in high school and college, and is presently an associate professor in the General Program of Liberal Studies at Notre Dame; he serves as poetry editor of *Critic* and editor of *Choice*, and gives frequent lectures and poetry readings across the country. His short stories, his criticism, and above all his poetry have appeared widely in literary magazines, and two collections have been published: *Cycle for Mother Cabrini* (Grove, 1955) and *Ghosts of the Heart* (University of Chicago, 1960). Mr. Logan lives with his wife and nine children in South Bend, Indiana.

February, 1963

A NOTE ON THE TYPE

THIS BOOK is set in ELECTRA, a Linotype face designed by W. A. *Dwiggins* (1880-1956). This face cannot be classified as either modern or old-style. It is not based on any historical model, nor does it echo any particular period or style. It avoids the extreme contrasts between thick and thin elements that mark most modern faces, and attempts to give a feeling of fluidity, power, and speed.

Composed, printed, and bound by
The Haddon Craftsmen, Inc., Scranton, Pa.
Typography and binding design by
VINCENT TORRE